Ramayana Tales
for Children

J.M. Mehta

An Imprint of V&S PUBLISHERS

Published by:

An Imprint of

F-2/16, Ansari Road, Daryaganj, New Delhi-110002
☎ 011-23240026, 011-23240027 • *Fax:* 011-23240028
Email: info@vspublishers.com • *Website:* www.vspublishers.com

Branch : Hyderabad
5-1-707/1, Brij Bhawan (Beside Central Bank of India Lane)
Bank Street, Koti, Hyderabad - 500 095
☎ 040-24737290
E-mail: vspublishershyd@gmail.com

Follow us on:

For any assistance sms **VSPUB** to **56161**

All books available at **www.vspublishers.com**

© **Copyright:** V&S PUBLISHERS
ISBN 978-93-505708-2-1
Edition 2014

The Copyright of this book, as well as all matter contained herein (including illustrations) rests with the Publishers. No person shall copy the name of the book, its title design, matter and illustrations in any form and in any language, totally or partially or in any distorted form. Anybody doing so shall face legal action and will be responsible for damages.

Printed at : Param Offseters, Okhla, New Delhi-110020

publisher's note

The story of Ramayana has been written in various Indian languages with different interpretations. It has been told, retold and translated in numerous Asian and European languages. V&S Publishers has compressed the whole epic through 40 one-page stories so that children can conveniently connect without losing track with innumerable characters.

The characters Ram, Sita, Lakshman, Bharat, Shatrughan, Hanuman and Ravan are all fundamental to the ethos, social mores and cultural consciousness of India, and also of South-east Asia.

With captivating caricature type illustrations spread throughout, the book will surely captivate the interest of children and retain their focus at all times.

An ideal book for every home!

We would be glad to receive feedback from parents to help us improve editorial and production standard.

Contents

Introduction 7
1. Dashrath the King of Ayodhya 9
2. Birth of Four Princes 11
3. Vishwamira Takes away Ram and Lakshman 13
4. Ahalya and Ram 15
5. The Origin of Sita 17
6. Swayamber of Sita 19
7. Dashrath Decides to Retire 21
8. Two Boons of Queen Kaikeyi 23
9. Ram's Departure to the Forest 25
10. How Dashrath Killed Shravan & Death of Dashrath ... 27
11. Return of Bharat & Shatrughan 29
12. Bharat Goes to Forest to Bring Back Rama 31
13. Ram and Sage Agastya 33
14. Visit of Soopnakha to Panchvati 35
15. Ravan Seeks Help of Mareech 37
16. Ravan Kidnaps Sita 39
17. Ram Meets Shabri 41
18. Ram Meets Hanuman and Sugreev 43
19. Pavan Putra Hanuman 45
20. Fight Between Sugreev and Baali 47
21. Search for Sita with Sugreev's Help 49
22. Hanuman is Captured 51
23. Hanuman's Tail Set on Fire 53
24. Hanuman Meets Ram 55

25. Attack on Lanka 57
26. Ravan Sends Kumbhakaran 59
27. Indrajit Attacks Ram's Army 61
28. Ravan Comes to Fight 63
29. Crowing of Vibhishan 65
30. Ram Returns to Ayodhya 67
31. Derogatory Remarks of Washerman 69
32. Ram Sends Sita to Exile 71
33. Sita Lives in the Hermitage of Sage Valmiki 73
34. Ashvamedha Yajna 75
35. Fight with Ram's Soldiers 77
36. Lav Kush Face Ram 79
37. Sita Meets Hanuman 81
38. Sita Returns to Mother Earth 83
39. Ram Wishes to Leave the World 85
40. Ram Leaves the World 87

introduction

The RAMAYANA is the most popular and famous epic of ancient INDIA. The word Ramayana means the life story of RAM who was the eldest son of DASHRATH, King of AYODHYA. The original work was written in SANSKRIT by MAHARISHI VALMIKI later on it was written in HINDI in verse by saint TULSI DAS under the popular name of 'RAMCHARIT MANAS'. It describes in detail the character, qualities and achievements of Lord RAM. Because of its ideal propositions and moral qualities Ramayana is held in highest esteem by people in India. It is considered a sacred book and its verses are devotional recited daily in most temples and Hindu homes. The popularity of Ramayana can be estimated by the fact that plays in the form of 'RAM KATHA' is being organized in different form in villages, cities not only in India but overseas as well. The most popular version of RAM KATHA by MORARI BAPU is broadcast live on T.V. channels and is watched by millions. RAMAYANA is also shown in the form of serial on the T.V. The recitation of verses of Ramayana brings joy and peace to devotees who sing these with utmost reverence and pure devotion.

ramayana

dashrath the king of ayodhya

DASHRATH belonged to the solar dynasty (SURYA VANSHA). This dynasty originated with MANU, The first ruler of humanity. Dashrath was the king of Ayodhya which is located on the bank of river Saryu. Dashrath was the grandson of the famous king Raghu after whom the solar dynasty later came to be known as Raghu Dynasty (Raghu Vansha)

Dashrath inherited good qualities of his great ancestors. He was very wealthy and strong. He vanquished his enemies easily. He was a person of great character and a popular ruler. He had three queens Kaushalya, Sumitra and Kaikeyi. Kaushalya was the eldest queen.

Although Dashrath was a strong and popular king yet he had one regret. He had no son to carry forward his dynasty. So one day he invited sage VASHISHTA to his court and expressed his wish saying ' I am very sad that I have no son. Thus I shall have no successor when I pass away and the solar dynasty will end with me. Please advise me what should be done.

Saga Vashistha who was a man of great foresight and spiritual vision advised the king to organize a YAJNA to be performed by a particular RISHI named SRINGA. Dashrath went to that rishi and invited him to Ayodhya to perform the yajna. The rishi came and performed the yajna which went on for full one year. At the end of the yajna a supernatural being emerged from the fire of yajna. He had a bowl in his hands. The figure gave the bowl to the king Dashrath and said 'Here is Prasad (Kheer) from the gods for your wives. If they eat they will bear four brilliant sons for you'

King Dashrath took the bowl and was overjoyed.

ramayana

5
birth of four princes

Rishi Sringa advised Dashrath that his queens should eat the kheer prasad so that they will bear children. This was done and in due course four children were born. KAUSHALYA, the eldest wife gave birth to RAM the eldest son. Second queen KAIKEYI gave birth to BHARAT and SUMITRA gave birth to LAKSHMAN and SHATRUGHAN. All the queen and the king become very happy. Rama the eldest son was born on the ninth day of the bright half of the sacred month CHAITRA. Besides the happy parents, the whole of Ayodhya was full of great joy at the birth of princes.

King Dashrath who was a great archer taught the art of archery to his brave sons. Later on they were sent to the hermitage (ashram) of sage VASHISTH for their formal education. He was a learned guru and a man of great knowledge and realization. Under his guidance all the four princes learned various arts and disciplines and were endowed with virtue and wisdom in due course. When their education was complete all four princes returned to the palace. Their parents and the people were delighted to see them. There was great rejoicing everywhere on their return to Ayodhya.

While in Ayodhya, Rama the crown prince taught his brothers how to be virtuous and also guided them in the matters of kingdom and society at large. He set his own example in observing the norms for the welfare of society. King Dashrath was happy to see his four sons grow up as brave vituous boys and popular in public.

ramayana

3

Vishwamira takes away Ram and Lakshman

One day a renowned sage VISHWAMITRA came to king Dashrath who welcomed the sage and said I am truly blessed by your visit. Is there anything I can do for you? The sage was glad to hear this and said 'While performing a yajna two dreadful demons, Mareech and Subahu troubled me a lot. My troubles will end if you send with me RAM your eldest son who can kill all demons.

Dashrath felt perplexed on hearing this demand and stood speechless with fear and anxiety. However sage Vashisth advised the king not to fear and send Rama along with Lakshman with Vishwamitra. King Dashrath agreed and Vishwamitra took both the princes to a dense forest. The sage warned both the princes about Tadka and her son Mareecha the ferocious demons had made the life of the people miserable. He prompted them to kill the demons. In the forest the battle began between Tadka and the princes. Ram killed Tadka. Vishwamitra embraced Ram and blessed him and felt happy.

ramayana

4

ahalya and ram

AHALYA was a woman of great beauty created by BRAHMA. Attracted by her beauty INDRA, the highest among gods wanted to many her. BRAHMA ignored him and left the girl in the care of sage GAUTAM.

As she grew up Brahma asked Gautam to marry her as he alone deserved to be her husband. They were married and lived happily. Meanwhile Indra who could not forget her waited for an opportunity to entice her. He came to know that Gautam would leave ashram early morning daily to go to the river for bath and prayer. Accordingly he planned to get hold of Ahalya by any means foul or fair.

One day Indra made the sage wakeup earlier by assuming the voice of a rooster. So Indra went away quite early that day. As the sage left, Indra disguised as Gautam entered the hut and made love to Ahalya who thought he was her husband. Meanwhile Gautam felt that something was wrong at the hut so he hurried back to find the couple in bed. Seeing Gautam Ahalya was shocked and ashamed. Indra assumed the form of a cat and ran away. Gautam cursed both as a result of which a thousand female marks appeared on the body of the cat and Ahalya turned into a stone. This happened despite her desperation and request for forgiveness. The sage also felt sorry and said nothing can be done now.

Indra's plight was heightened and he remained disturbed. This caused concern to other gods who intervened and requested Brahma to approach Gautam who in response to Brahma's appeal converted thousand marks into eyes. Thus Indra became a god with thousand eyes.

Later when Vishwamitra and Ram passed that way Ram's feet touched the stone half sunk in the ground. The stone was instantly transformed into a beautiful women. Vishwamitra introduced her to Ram and told about sage Gautam and his curse and the whole story of Ahalya.

Ram said to her "May you join your husband and live with him again. You need not burden your heart with what has happened and passed over." This is how Ahalya was redeemed.

5

the origin of sita

While travelling in his Pushpak Viman over the Himalayas RAVAN, the great king of Lanka spotted an ascetic girl engaged in intense meditation as she looked very. Ravan, overcome by lust approached her and said 'O' beautiful lady, this solitary life of meditation is a mismatch to your youth and beauty. Please tell me who you are and why are you meditating.

The girl treated Ravan as a respectable guest and said I am daughter of a great Mother Earth. I was born as a spiritual child to my learned and virtuous father Janak. My name is VEDA VATI. When I grew up several youngmen asked for my hand. My father refused as he wanted VISHNU as his son in law. She further said 'Once a Rakshas named SHAMBHU saw me and approached my father for my hand. As my father refused, Shambhu killed my father while he was fast asleep. Overcome by great grief my mother killed herself by entering into the burning pyre of my father'. I have decided to fulfill the wishes of my father to have Vishnu as his son in law and have Vishnu as my husband. That is why I am engaged in intense meditation. Ravan tried to persuade her not to waste her youth in that ascetic living. Full of vanity and pride he said I am the great king of Lanka. I will make you my queen. And tell me who is Vishnu Is he equal to me in power and splendor? Ved Vati said, the whole world bows before Vishnu who is the Lord of the world.

Ravan enraged by these words caught her by her hair. This shocked Ved Vati and using her hand as a sword she cut her hair in one stroke. Only a bunch of her hair remained in the hand of Ravan. Ved Vati scolded Ravan and said" You have insulted me. As I have no desire to live any longer. I shall immediately immolate myself. I will be born again and be the reason for your death. I shall be born to highly virtuous parents as a spiritual offspring. After saying these words she caught fire through her will power and immolated herself instantly. Ved Vati was born as a baby in the stem of a lotus flower in her next birth. Somehow Ravan got hold of this beautiful new born girl and brought her in his place. However astrologers told him that the presence of this girl in his place would be dangerous and could cause his death. So they advised him to throw her away and Ravan did so.

It is believed that in due cause of time the same girl was found by King Janak who was ploughing in a corn field in his kingdom. She became the daughter of king Janak who named her SITA. She married RAM (who was incarnation of VISHNU) and became the cause of death of Ravan the king of Lanka.

Swayamber of Sita

Vishwamitra along with Rama and Lakshman went to Mithila, the capital of king JANAK. He welcomed them. The swayamber of Janak's daughter SITA was being organized at that time. King Janak took them to the site of the ceremony where the bow of Lord SHIVA was placed for trial by the princes and kings who had arrived from all parts of India to win the hand of Sita.

The bow of Lord Shiva was so heavy and strong that no one could lift it. This disappointed King Janaka. At this, sage, Vishwamitra exhorted Ram to break the bow. Ram moved toward the bow with great confidence and lifted it easily and broke the bow into two pieces. The huge noise produced by the breaking of Lord Shiva's bow attracted the attention of PARSHURAM. He came there. In rage he spoke harsh words "O, Janak tell me who has broken the bow?" Janak was very much terrified. Ram intervened with folded hands and pacified Parshuram. After this, Sita garlanded Ram as her husband. When this news reached Ayodhya, Dashrath came to Mithila with his followers for the wedding ceremony. The marriage ceremony of Ram and Sita was performed with great pomp and show. At the same time, Lakshman was married to URMILA the younger sister of Sita. King Janak's brother had two beautiful daughters, Mandavi and Shrutikirte who were also married to prince Bharat and prince Shatrughan respectively on the some occasion.

After the wedding king Dashrath returned to Ayodhya with his four sons and their newly wedded wives. They were all given a warm reception by the citizens of Ayodhya. The whole city was decorated. The queens welcomed their sons and daughters in law at the palace and were full of happiness.

Ramayana

5

dashrath decides to retire

All the princes and their brides lived happily thereafter for many years. Considering his old age king Dashrath wished to crown Ram as his successor. He consulted sage. The entire assembly declared with one voice that Ram should be crowned as he was an idol of the people. Ram was informed and the day of coronation was fixed. All were very happy.

Meanwhile Manthara the personal servant of queen Kaikeyi conspired and advised her to protest against Ram's coronation. Manthara asked Kaikeyi to seek redemption of two boons promised by the king sometime earlier. According to these Kaikeyi's son Bharat must be crowned and Ram should be exiled for 14 years. Kaikeyi was so much influenced by Manthara that she immediately protested. When Dashrath came to know about it he was horrified to see the determination of his queen who was obstinate and sought fulfilment of boons.

The story goes that Long ago king Dashrath had got injured and in good faith queen Kaikeyi had saved his life. At that time the king had granted her two boons. Kaikeyi asked the king to grant these boons now. The king had no choice but to to the proposal and Kaikeyi had put forward before the king.

ramayana

8
two boons of queen kaikeyi

When king Dashrath agreed to grant two boons to Kaikeyi promised by him earlier she become bold and put forward her two demands as follows:-
    1. My first demand is crown my son Bharat.
    2. My second demand is exile Ram to live in forest for 14 years.

Hearing these harsh and unexpected demands king Dashrath was horrified and fell down unconscious. When he recovered he begged Kaikeyi not to banish Ram to the forest but she did not agree and insisted upon sending Ram to the forest without delay. Ram was soon called in the presence of king and the queen who informed him about her two demands. Ram had no hesitation in conveying his willingness to go to the forest. He informed his mother Kaushlya about it without showing any sign of sorrow. Lakshman and Sita both got ready to accompany Ram to the forest. The three went to the king to meet him and seek his blessings.

ramayana

5
Ram's departure to the forest

Ram, Sita and Lakshman came out of the palace to go to the forest. It was a heart rending scene as the people of Ayodhya followed their chariot sobbing and weeping bitterly. King Dashrath who saw them leaving moaned and fell down. Their chariot stopped on the bank of river TAMSA for night stay. They crossed the river next day early morning and after crossing many streams they reached the banks of river GANGA. Here the boatman washed the feet of Lord Ram and then took them across the river in his boat.

Next day they went to the hermitage of sage Bhardwaj who embraced Ram and advised them that Chitrakoot would be the ideal place for them to stay.

15

how dashrath killed shravan & death of dashrath

After the departure of Ram to the forest the condition of Dashrath became worse with grief. In order to share his grief he told queen Kaushalya about the horrible sin he had committed in his youth by killing Shravan the only son of blind parents.

Dashrath was an accomplished archer. He could hit invisible targets aiming by sounds only. One night he went out to hunt on the banks of river Saryu. It was dense dark and he waited for some wild animal to come. Suddenly he heard a sound as if same animal was drinking water. He shot an arrow in that direction and was horrified to hear a human voice crying in great pain. When he went to that place he saw that his arrow had pierced through the body of a young boy who lay in a pool of blood. That boy was SHRAVAN who cried "O God you have killed me. My blind parents are lying thirsty some distance away. Take this pitcher of water to them but do not tell them anything about my condition." Thereafter Shravan expired. Taking the pitcher to the blind parents the king fell at their feet and confessed how he had killed their son. The blind parents plunged into great grief and tears rolled down their eyes. Dashrath carried them to the place where their dead son lay dead. When the funeral pyre of their son was lit they jumped into and burnt themselves alive. While doing so they cursed Dashrath that he too would die grieving for his son as they were dying.

The curse of blind parents of Shravan haunted king Dashrath. In great grief he cried for his son Ram. A few days after the departure of Ram, king Dashrath breathed his last. The whole palace and the city plunged into gloom. All the queen wept bitterly. Sage Vashishth arrived soon and messengers were sent to bring Bharat and Shatrughan who had gone out of Ayodhya.

This is the brief story of killing of Shravan by king Dashrath and his own death.

return of bharat & shatrughan

At the call of sage Vashishth, Bharat and Shatrughan returned to Ayodhya a few days after the death of king Dashrath. The city wore a deserted look. They did not find their father at the palace. When Bharat met queen Kaikeyi he enquired about his father, Ram, Sita and Lakshman. He became furious when he knew about them. Shatrughan kicked Manthara for her dirty job. Bharat got angry at her mother. Sage Vashishth consoled both princes and prepared them to perform the funeral rites of their departed father. The funeral pyre was lit on the banks of river Saryu and the remains of king Dashrath were consigned to flames with Vedic chants. After the ceremony Bharat and others bathed in the river and offered prayers for the departed soul.

ramayana

12

Bharat goes to forest to bring back Rama

After the mourning period was over the ministers called the Assembly. It was decided to crown Bharat as the king of Ayodhya. Bharat did not accept this proposal and suggested that they should go to the forest to bring back Ram and crown him as the king. All admired this suggestion. Bharat accompanied by court people sages and three mothers went to the forest to bring back Ram. A huge army followed them for their protection. Hearing the noise and cloud of dust Lakshman climbed up a tree and was alarmed to see a big army advancing towards their hut. Keeping the army some distance away, Bharat accompanied by Shatrughan and sage Vashishth came to the cottage. He met Ram and fell at his feet. Ram embraced him. Hearing about father's death Ram was greatly shocked. All the ministers, sages and princes pleaded with Ram to return to Ayodhya but he did not agree as he had to obey his father's command. Therefore Bharat asked for wooden sandals of Ram and said the sandles shall rule over Ayodhya till his return. Ram agreed and Bharat returned to Ayodhya with all the people.

13
ram and sage agastya

After the departure of Bharat, Ram left Chitrakoot. He went to the hermitage of sage Agastya who welcomed them with great affection. Sage Agastya was a man of great ability and vision. He knew about the mission of Ram and gave him powerful weapons to kill the demons. He also advised them to live at PANCHVATI. They built a cottage there and started living peacefully. On their way to Panchvati they also saw a huge creature perched on a big tree. It was JATAYU, who offered himself to protect SITA in the absence of Ram and Lakshman. Ram, Lakshman and Sita lived peacefully among natural beauty and close to saints and sages for about ten years. In the company of Ram and Lakshman the sages were free from the fear of demons.

14

Visit of Soopnakha to Panchvati

One morning after taking bath in the river GODAVARI the three were sitting outside their cottage. Suddenly Soopnakha, sister of RAVAN came there. Seeing the grace and beauty of Ram, she fell in love with him and proposed to marry him. Ram told her that he was already married and therefore she should propose to Lakshman. So she proposed to Lakshman who ignored her and told her to ask Ram to take her as his second wife. She was enraged at the sight of Sita and was about to attack her when Ram saved Sita. He told Lakshman to teach Soopnakha a lesson. Lakshman took up his sword and chopped off her nose. Bleeding and mad with pain she rushed to her brothers Khara and Dooshna. They came to avenge their sister's plight with a huge army of demons. The battle began but Ram alone defeated their enemy.

ramayana

15

Ravan Seeks Help of Mareech

SOOPNAKHA bleeding and injured came to Ravan and apprised him of her plight. She prompted him to kidnap Sita to avenge her insult. Ravan became furious and his lust for beautiful Sita was also aroused. So he sought the help of Mareech who was strong and had magical powers. Both made a plan to kidnap Sita. Mareech and Ravan both went to the forest where Ram and Sita lived accompanied by Lakshman. Mareech transformed himself into a wonderful golden deer of great beauty. When Sita saw the deer she asked Ram and Lakshman to catch the deer for her. In order to fulfil the desire of Sita, Ram went after the deer who ran away. He asked Lakshman to be with Sita and take care of her.

Mareech in the form of deer ran far away so that Ravan could get sufficient time to kidnap Sita. Ram shot an arrow which pierced the deer and Mareech assumed his human form. He imitated the voice of Ram and cried Ah Sita, Ah Lakshman and fell dead. Hearing Ram's cry for help Sita instructed Lakshman to run at once and help his brother. Before leaving he drew a line around the hut and asked Sita not to cross it. This was done as he feared that some unforeseen may happen in his absence. So Lakshman left the hut and went away.

ramayana

16

ravan kidnaps sita

When Ram and Lakshman were away from the hut Ravan came there in the guise of a sage. He asked Sita for alms. As soon as she came out of the hut with some fruits and crossed the line Ravan cought hold of her and took her away in his chariot. She cried and Jatayu came to her help but he was seriously injured. Meanwhile Ram had killed the golden deer which turned into Mareech. Ram realized that the demons had deceived him. He hurried back to hut and met Lakshman on the way. Seeing Lakshman, Ram cried why did you have Sita alone? Lakshman narrated the circumstances in which he had to leave Sita because of her insistence to go and help Ram. Ram cried in vain in great sorrow and Lakshman tried to console him. On their way back they were horrified to see Jatayu lying in a pool of blood and groaning with great pain. Ram took him in his lap. Jatayu told Ram that Ravan had carried Sita away and how he got wounded while fighting him. Jatayu was alive only to tell Ram what he knew.

ramayana

17

Ram meets Shabri

Ram and Lakshman moved from place to place in search of Sita. As they moved forward they arrived at the hut of aged SHABRI who was the disciple of sage Matanga. She was overjoyed to see Ram and fed them with delicious fruits. Shabri was full of purity of mind almost to the point of devotion. Ram told her that you are innocent like a child. You are blessed. Shabri had lived a life of pure love and devotion. After meeting Ram and seeking his blessing she gained salvation.

ramayana

18
ram meets hanuman and sugreev

Ram and Lakshman march continued their forward searching for Sita. When they came near Rishyamook Mountain, the Vanar king SUGREEV got alarmed to see them as he thought that his elder brother BAALI had sent them to kill him. Sugreev asked his companion HANUMAN to go and find out who they were. Hanuman went to see and met them. He came to know about them and why they had come there. Hanuman fell at the feet of Ram and told him about Sugreev. He took them both to Sugreev. After talking to each other they became friends and decided to help each other. Sugreev told Ram about the treatments of his elder brother Baali who had snatched his kingdom. Ram promised to help him. Sugreev offered his help in searching Sita. Thus a bond of friendship was established between Ram and Sugreev. Sugreev showed Ram some ornaments thrown from the sky by a weeping woman. Lakshman recognized these ornaments as anklet of Sita as he often saw them while touching Sita's feet. However he was not familiar with other ornaments worn by Sita as he never looked at Sita's face.

ramayana

pavan putra hanuman

The great warrior HANUMAN is said to have been born through the blessing of wind god. That is why he is also known as PAVAN PUTRA or PAVAN Sut or the son of wind god. Her mother was ANJANI and his natural father KESARI was the king of SUMERU mountainous region. Baby Hanuman was very strong and powerful. One morning when Hanuman was fast asleep his mother went out in the garden to get some fruit. After sometime Hanuman woke up. When he looked out through the window he saw the orange coloured rising son and thought it was a ripe fruit. He jumped out to catch it. Wind god anticipated the danger of Hanuman being burnt. He assumed the form of a snow mountain. The sun god also saw Hanuman. Rahu at that moment also wanted to eat the sun but Hanuman attacked and Rahu fled away. He straight went to INDRA and complained that someone else was trying to eat sun which was his food. So Indra came rushing to the scene. When Hanuman saw Indra, he left the sun god and ran after Rahu. Indra hit Hanuman with a strong weapon. Hanuman fell unconscious on a rockey mountain. Seeing this the wind God picked up Hanuman and took him to a safe place. The wind - god became furious and refused to maintain cosmic order. Consequently air flow stopped and it became difficult to breathe. So all gods went to BRAHMA for help. Brahma came to the wind god who placed the body of Hanuman at the feet of Brahma and sought his blessing. Brahma blessed the baby who smiled and came back to life. Brahma then spoke to all and told them about the greatness of Hanuman. Lord Indra and all other gods blessed Hanuman. The wind god took Hanuman to Anjani and informed her all about these happenings. Hanuman he did lot of mischief to the annoyance of Rishis who complained to Anjani and Kesari. Rishi's declared "O' Hanuman from now onwards you will forgot about your real strength which has become the cause of all your mischief. You will get it back when you become adult. Till then you will remain calm.

20

Fight Between Sugreev and Baali

BAALI had snatched the kingdom of Sugreev and driven him away to the mountain. He had also deprived Sugreev of his family. Sugreev wanted to have his kindom and family back. Ram was ready to help Sugreev in this venture. They all went to Kishkindha with a plan. While Ram stood behind a big tree in the nearby forest he asked Sugreev to challenge Baali to come out of the palace and fight with him. The two brothers started fighting. Ram was unable to distinguish from a distance and therefore could not shoot at Baali. Since Baali was stronger he wounded Sugreev who fled for his life and complained to Ram for not helping him. Ram told him the reason and put a garland around his neck in order to distinguish him so Sugreev went again and challenged Baali for another fight. Baali's wife Tara asked Baali to refrain from fighting but he did not agree. As the two brothers were fighting Ram saw Sugreev in trouble and therefore shot an arrow which pierced Baali's chest. This is how Baali was killed and Sugreev regained his kingdom.

ramayana

21

Search for Sita with Sugreev's help

Thereafter intensive search for Sita began with the help of Hanuman, Sugreev and his army. They spread in different directions. After long search they came to know that Ravan had captured Sita and confined her in the Ashok Vatika of LANKA and that she was well – guarded by many demons. In order to go to Lanka, they had to cross the sea. Blessed with divine power and strength, Hanuman crossed the sea and reached Lanka. After great efforts and roaming around, Hanuman found Sita sitting under a tree in the Ashok Vatika of Ravan. She was thin and pale, in tears and surrounded by demons.

Ravan tried to woo Sita with all sorts of temptations but he could not win her love and was greatly disappointed. Meanwhile Hanuman found an opportunity to meet her alone. He told her that he was a messenger from Ram and also showed her Ram's ring in order to win her confidence. He encouraged Sita not to grieve anymore and assured her that soon Ram and Lakshman with huge army would attack Lanka. After taking leave of Sita, Hanuman went around Ashok Vatika to eat sweet fruits. Having satisfied his hunger, he uprooted many trees and killed many demons, who had come to catch him.

Ramayana

22

Hanuman is Captured

When the news of destruction of Ashok Vatika reached Ravan he became furious. First he sent his son Aksha and his army. Thereafter, Ravan sent his son Indrajeet also who was a great warrior. A terrible battle raged between the two great warriors. After a furious fight Hanuman was captured and taken to Ravan's court bound wih the ropes. Ravan enquired who he was and Hanuman informed him that he was a messenger of Ram. Hanuman told Ravan that kidnapping of Sita was an evil act and he should return Sita back to Ram and seek his forgiveness. He also warned Ravan that he would face death and destruction if he did not do this. Hearing Hanuman's warning, Ravan lost his temper and ordered his instant death. But his brother Vibhishan intervened and observed that a messenger must not be killed. He therefore ordered that Hanuman's tail should be set on fire and he should be beaten hard.

23

Hanuman's tail set on fire

As ordered by Ravan, Hanuman's tail was wrapped in all kinds of rags and elongated. The end of the very long tail was dipped in oil and set on fire. He was then taken through the street and mocked by the people. When Sita learnt about this, she prayed to god for his safety. Hanuman endured all this insult. Then suddenly he shrank in size and broke off all the ropes that bound him. Thereafter he jumped with his blazing tail on the top of the buildings and set them on fire. In this way he jumped from house to house and set the whole city on fire. A strong wind engulfed the whole city in flames. The city of Lanka was reduced to ashes. Then he jumped into the sea and the fire in his tail was extinguished. He then went to Sita who was happy to see him safe and without harm. He then sought her permission to go back and left Lanka.

Ramayana

24

Hanuman Meets Ram

On return from Lanka, Hanuman briefed Ram about the plight of Sita. He told Ram how she missed him and prayed for him despite being in great agony. Ram thanked Hanuman for his heroic deed. He began planning to rescue Sita. Sugreev offered his help and started preparations to go to Lanka. Ram and Sugreev with a huge army reached the sea shore. Having reached the sea shore they wondered how to cross the sea. The huge army of Sugreev went into the extensive forest and brought rocks, trees, boulders and dragged them to the sea and filled the sea step by step. Within a few days a bridge was built across the sea. Meanwhile Vibhishan the younger brother of Ravan to kill him also took refuge at the feet of Ram. Ravan was angry with Vibhishan because the latter had advised the former to restore Sita to Ram. Ram welcomed Vibhishan with open arms and promised protection.

25

attack on lanka

After crossing sea and reaching Lanka, Ram ordered immediate attack and besieged the city from all sides. The soldiers rushed towards the city and killed demons wherever they met them. Ravan sent a huge army to face Ram's army. A furious battle began between the two armies. Soldiers were killed in thousands on both sides. The first day of the battle was furious. Indrajeet the most valiant son of Ravan, made himself invisible by magic and shot arrow at Ram and Lakshman who found themselves helpless as they did not know from where the arrows were coming. Both were wounded by arrows and fell down unconscious. This led to great panic in Ram's camp. Ravan was very happy when Indrajeet told him that he had killed both Ram and Lakshman. But Ram and Lakshman had not died. They had become unconscious for a while but soon revived and stood up to the rejoicing of their companions. Soon they got ready to attack the army of Ravan. At the news of their fresh attack, Ravan was greatly shocked. Filled with greatly anxiety and burning with rage. Ravan rushed to the battlefield. He caused immense destruction in the battlefield and even Lakshman fell unconscious. Then Ram went forward to confront Ravan. His sharp arrows wounded Ravan and his chariot was smashed into pieces. He was bleeding profusely. He was helpless. He was fatigued. Raman took pity on him and said 'you have fought bravely but lost. As you are wounded, tired and helpless go home and come back tomorrow to fight again.' Ravan had no option but to retreat to his palace in great shame.

ramayana

26

ravan sends kumbhakaran

After defeat by Ram, Ravan sought the help of his younger brother Kumbhakaran who had gone into deep sleep. When he was aroused with great efforts Ravan told him about his defeat and destruction of Lanka at the hands of Ram and his huge army. Kumbhakaran consoled his brother and resolved to kill Ram and Lakshman. Armed with his mighty weapons he marched to the battlefield followed by an army to help him. Kumbhakaran was a mighty warrior. He struck down Angad and Sugreev and rushed towards Ram's camp. None could stop him on the way. Ram faced him and cut off his legs with sharp and powerful arrows which ultimately killed Kumbhakaran. When Ravan came to know about the killing of Kumbhakaran he groaned in grief. These was great joice in Ram's camp. Full of great enthusiasm Ram's army attacked demons and killed them in thousands.

27

Indrajit attacks Ram's army

When Ravan suffered defeat by Ram's army he had to face great ignominy. His brave son Indrajit comforted him and resolved to destroy Ram's army. He launched a massive attack but faced stiff resistance. Then he attacked Lakshman with his might weapon "Brahmastra" Which was considered indestructible. It pierced Lakshman's body who fell down seriously injured and became unconscious. This caused great gloom in Ram's camp. Hanuman was assigned the task of bringing the curative herb called SANJIVANI which could cure Lakshman. As soon as the drug was administered to him he became conscious and got up with renewed energy and vigour. Ram embraced him warmly. Lakshman then accompanied by his great warrior chased Indrajit who had gone to his mountain hide out. A long and fierce battle was raged between Lakshman and Indrajit. At last Lakshman shot the fatal arrow and cut off the head of Indrajit. In this way Indrajit the bravest warrior son of Ravan lost his life and Ravan was deprived of his right hand man.

28

Ravan Comes to Fight

After Indrajit was slain, Ravan had no option but to come to the battlefield. He came in his strong and swift chariot accompanied by his powerful army. He attacked Ram's army with great force and caused great damage. Ravan's attack was faced with great strength by Ram's army. Hanuman killed thousands of demons. Ram's powerful arrows caused have among Ravan's army. Great warriors of Rama's army, like Hanuman, Sugreev, Angad, and many others fought with great vigour and bravery. Consequently there was death and destruction all around in the camp of Ravan. When most of the great warriors of Ravan's army including his sons and relatives and thousands of demon soldiers were killed Ravan came face to face with Ram. He urged his commanders to kill Ram and defeat his army. Ram and Lakshman accompanied by Vibhishan went ahead to face Ravan. Their soldiers also rushed forward with great vigour and enthusiasm. As they marched forward, they crushed all resistance which came their way. Soon Ram flooded the battlefield with arrows in all directions Ravan attacked Ram with his arrow which were rendered useless. Meanwhile Ram was advised to use the greatest weapon 'Brahmastra' to kill Ravan as he could not be killed by any other weapon. Ram shot the great weapon at Ravan which pierced his chest and the great demon king fell down dead. This is how Ravan who considered himself invincible met his doom at the hands of Ram.

Ramayana

29

Crowing of Vibhishan

Vibhishan, brother of Ravan had already joined the camp of Ram because of his differences with his elder brother. But when he saw the dead body of his brother, he burst into tears. Ram consoled him and asked him to perform the last rites of his dead brother. When the funeral ceremony was over, Ram, Lakshman and Vibhishan accompanied by Hanuman, Sugreev, and others all went to Lanka. Vibhishan was then made to sit in the throne with due honour and respect. Ram crowned him as king. Hanuman was sent to Ashoka Vatika to meet Sita and to inform her about the victory of Ram's army over Ravan. Sita was overjoyed to hear this news. Sita was brought to Ram who wanted to test her purity as she had remained in Ravan's captivity. She went through the fiery ordeal but came out unharmed. Ram was pleased to see her and accepted her as his inseparable companion.

ramayana

30

Ram Returns to Ayodhya

After completing exile of fourteen years, Ram, Sita and Lakshman returned to Ayodhya, where Bharat and people of Ayodhya were waiting for them eagerly. The entire city was decorated like a bride. Sage Vashisht ahead of all the people welcomed them and embraced them with great love. Bharat fell on the feet of Ram who lifted him and embraced him. Sage Vashisth called meeting of the assembly and proposed that Ram should occupy the royal throne. All agreed with great delight in one voice. Both Ram and Sita dressed in royal clothes and jewels were seated in the royal throne amidst the chants of vedic mantras. The sages, the learned priests, the court official and all others present were overjoyed to see this ceremony. The queen mothers were delighted. The sages blessed Ram, the rightful owner of the royal throne. Gifts were given to priests and donations were made to all the needy people who were fully satisfied. Thus Ram became the king of Ayodhya.

ramayana

३१

derogatory remarks of washerman

Sometime after the coronation of Ram as king, he got reports from people some of which were good and some bad. Citizen talked about brave deeds of Ram and admired him but there was also some unpleasant remarks by some people about the purity of Sita who remained in the captivity of wicked Ravan who might have polluted her. Ram knew about the purity of Sita but these unpleasant remarks by some citizen perturbed him. One day Ram was told about some bitter remarks made about Sita by a petty washerman. The story is like this that a washerman was heard saying to his wife who spent night outside "O, where, where did you spend last night? I cannot keep you any more I am not like Ram who accepted his wife Sita even though she had lived with Ravan for many years. Ram was greatly aggrieved to hear these derogatory remarks of the washerman and began thinking about appropriate action.

32

Ram sends Sita to exile

After much thinking Ram called his brother and shared his thought with them. He spokes to them in a depressed tone as follows:-

"Dear brother, you are the sum and substance of my life. You are also the well- wisher of the people. I therefore share my problem with you. While I consider Sita as a pure and noble person, the common citizen of Ayodhya have different opinion and speak poorly about her. They fear that their wives could also live with others for some time and then return home. As a king I cannot ignore such aspersions. Therefore after much thinking I have decided to send Sita to exile. Ram then instructed to take Sita in a chariot and leave her in the forest across Ganga near the hermitage of sage Valmiki. Next morning Lakshman did so. Sita was fearful but Lakshman explained the circumstances which led to their sad situation. Hearing that she had been forsaken by the king, she fell unconscious. When Sita recovered, She spoke to Lakshman:

I was created to suffer. I feel miserable but what sin has been committed by me? I cannot end my life as I carry a baby in my womb, the descendant of my Lord Ram. Let Lord Ram conduct himself in such a way that the citizen of Ayodhya do not cast any aspersion on him. This duty is dearer to me than my own life. Lakshman you have to do as ordered by him. May god bless you, Hearing Sita's agony Lakshman paid his respect to her and took leave of her to return to Ayodhya. While Sita cried alone in the forest.

Ramayana

33

Sita lives in the hermitage of sage Valmiki

As Sita was left near the hermitage of sage VALMIKI, his young sons spotted her when they came out of the hermitage. They saw her weeping and informed their father. Soon Valmiki went and told her that he knows about her noble family and her purity because of his inner vision. He welcomed her and brought her to his hermitage to stay without fear. Valmiki consoled her in every way and Sita felt encouraged and assured when the ladies of the hermitage showered their love and affection upon her. During her stay in the hermitage Sita gave birth to two sons. They were named Lav and Kush by the sage who was greatly delighted to see and blessed both of them. Both boys grew up under the loving care of mother Sita and wise guidance of sage Valmiki. They respected and obeyed their mother and the guru. As they grew up sage Valmiki imparted them proper education and trained them in the art of archery and warfare. At the same time, the sage Valmiki who was busy writing Ramayana also guided them how to recite the story of Ram and Sita in a sweet voice.

Ramayana

34

ashvamedha yajna

Ram the king of Ayodhya decided to perform the ASHVAMEDHA YAJNA. This yajna is performed by a great king to establish and extend his rule over other distant region and to gain victory over any opposing rulers. All preparations were made to perform this yajna in the forest of NAIMISA, on the banks of holy river GOMTI. Messengers were sent in all directions to inform other kings and rulers to attend the yajna. All the great kings came and participated in the ceremony. They all brought presents for the king Ram to show their love and respect for him. The great yajna was performed amidst loud chants of Vedic mantra in the presence of a huge gathering of priests, king and the general public. After the ceremony food, drinks, clothing and other necessities of life were distributed among the needy. Gold, silver coins and jewels were also donated in large quantity. All who came to attend the yajna showered all praise for the grandest ceremony which they had ever witnessed. After the completion of the yajna a white horse was brought near the sacred fire. It was decorated fully and the king Ram applied Tilak in its forehead. A notice was hung around the neck. It read as follows:-

This horse belongs to KOSHALA EMPEROR RAMACHADRA. He who captures this horse shall have to wage a war with him. Those who accept his rule shall have to pay taxes imposed by him. The horse was accompanied by a army under the leadership of Shatrughan. As the horse and the army marched forward all kings on the way bowed before Shatrughan and accepted the lordship of great emperor Ram. They all agreed to pay the taxes. After a few days the horse passed through the forest where the hermitage of sage Valmiki was situated. Lav and Kush who saw the beautiful horse were fascinated and caught hold of it and tied it to a tree. They read the play card hung round to neck and waited for its owners to come.

ramayana

35

Fight with Ram's Soldiers

After sometime, Ram's soldiers arrived there in search of the ceremonial horse. They were surprised to see the horse tied to a tree and guarded by two hermit boys. The soldiers asked them to free the horse but they refused to do so. The soldiers then armed their arrows upon them. The two brothers retaliated and shot down a few soldiers while others fled away. The retreating soldiers informed Shatrughan. He came to the spot where the horse was tied. He was astonished to see the two loving boys and politely asked them to release the horse. Shatrughan told them the purpose of Ashwamegh Yagya. The boys instead indicated their readiness to fight. The Shatrughan picked up his bow and arrows. Lav and Kush quickly shot arrows and broke his chariot. Shatrughan became shot a valley of arrows at Lav and Kush and also ordered his other soldiers to attack them. A fierce battle ensued between the two sides. Shatrughan was seriously wounded and he fell down on the ground. The so-called gallant soldiers fled away to Ram and told him all about it. Ram instructed Lakshman to go to the forest. He advised him to capture the boys alive. When Lakshman went there and saw the two loving boys, he asked them to return the horse without fighting but they made fun of him. This enraged Lakshman. He shot a mighty arrow at Kush who was wounded and fell unconscious. Seeing this Lav sought guidance from his Guru. With his grace Kush revived immediately and got up to fight again. Lav shot an invincible arrow at Lakshman who fell down unconscious.

The soldiers left the battlefield to convoy the news to Ram. Bharat was called and ordered to go to the battlefield accompanied by Hanuman. Hanuman too could not defeat them. Bharat then shot a powerful arrow at Lav who fell to the ground. This angered Kush who shot a mighty arrow which pierced through Bharat's chest. He fell unconscious. After hearing the sad news of Bharat's fall Ram himself went to the battlefield accompanied by Vibhishan.

Ramayana

36

lav kush face ram

When Ram saw the two boys he was deeply attracted by them. He lovingly spoke to them, admired their valour and enquired about them and their parents. They told them what they knew about themselves, their mother and the sage Valmiki but they confessed ignorance about the identity of their father. Ram was overjoyed to see his glorious sons face to face. But the boys challenged Ram either to fight or to leave the horse and go away. Ram picked up his bow and the fight started. Ram deflected all arrows shot at him by the boys but himself did not shot a single arrow at them. Both the boys were puzzled at Ram's strange tactics. When Hanuman saw that Ram was not attacking the boys, he got angry and came to the battlefield to fight. Kush faced Hanuman and overpowered him and tied him with ropes. They then decided to take him away to the hermitage so that their mother may be delighted to see him.

ramayana

37

Sita meets Hanuman

When Hanuman was brought to the hermitage SITA was dumb founded to see him in that condition. But Hanuman was overjoyed to see mother Sita and touched her feet. He told her the whole story of the battle and the arrival of Ram. Sita was shocked to hear about the battle between her son and their father Ram. She went to sage Valmiki and shared her agony with him. It was a matter of great shame that sons were fighting against their father, she said to him. Valmiki knew everything because of his inner vision. The sage agreed with her and tried to console her by saying that she should not worry as all things will turn up to a better ending. The next day Lav and Kush again went to the battlefield. They challenged Ram and advised him not to fight and to return to his capital. However Ram advised them not to talk in such manner and return horse without fighting. The boys did not agree and started shooting arrows at Ram who made them ineffective. When Ram was about to shot an invincible arrow at the boys, the sage Valmiki appeared on the scene and tried to stop the fighting. Seeing the great sage Ram did not shot the arrow and fell at the feet of Valmiki who revealed to Ram that the two boys were his own sons. Ram was greatly surprised but also overjoyed to know this and he instantly embraced his dear sons. He blessed and they were also delighted to meet their father. Valmiki also informed Ram how both Lav and Kush were living there. Meanwhile Sita also arrived there. Ram was hesitant to express his delight because of the public opinion against her. Sita was perturbed to see such attitude of Ram but the sage Valmiki pacified her and advised her to return to Ayodhya with her sons and husband. She looked towards Ram who did not say anything and it seemed that he was still unwilling to take her back. The sage Valmiki assured Ram about the purity and chastity of Sita. But Ram as a king was afraid of the criticism of the people of Ayodhya. Sita therefore did not return to Ayodhya.

38

Sita Returns to Mother Earth

While Ram did not ask Sita to return to Ayodhya with him the other three brothers Lakshman, Bharat, and Shatrughan tried their best to persuade her to return to Ayodhya. But she refused as Lord Ram was hesitant to take her back. She was therefore full of sorrow. Dismayed and heart-broken she went to the banks of river Saryu and prayed to mother earth in great anguish. She exclaimed "O' Mother Earth, I worshipped Lord Ram in thought speech and action and never thought of any other man except Ram. "O Earth goddess please split and take me in your lap. It is believed that hearing Sita's plea full of pain and sorrow, lightning struck and thunder flashed and a great earthquake ripped the earth. A glorious throne arose from the earth and the earth goddess was sitting on it. The goddess welcomed her daughter with open arms and Sita went into her lap. The throne then went down into the earth and disappeared. The earth closed and became normal as it was before. The onlookers who kept on gazing with great astonishment and horror cried with tears rolling down their eyes. Lav and Kush wept bitterly and Ram was dumb founded to see Sita going into the womb of Mother Earth. Ram with his two sons and other companions returned to Ayodhya. He was given rousing reception. The whole city was well decorated and illuminated on the return of their beloved king. But Ram was sad in his heart as he felt the loss of Sita whom he loved and adored. He was therefore without peace of mind. After sometime the three queens had also passed away. Ram suffered great pain and sorrow.

ramayana

39

Ram wishes to leave the world

Having lived in Ayodhya for a long time Ram pondered over his life and its events. he realised that his life on this over earth should come to an end. Meanwhile Lord Vishnu called DHARM RAJA (God of Death) and said to him "O' God of death, as Lord Rama has completed his duty on Earth, please go to the earth and bring him back to heaven. Dharm Raja reached Ayodhya in the guise of a Brahman and met Lakshman at the gate of the palace and expressed his desire to meet Ram. Lakshman informed Ram accordingly. Lord Ram himself came out and took Brahman with him inside the palace. The Brahman revealed himself in his true form of Dharm Raja and conveyed the message of Lord Vishnu to Ram, who was much pleased to hear this. Ram then said I took human birth to serve the world. As my mission on earth has come to an end I am ready to return to heaven from where I had come. While Ram and Dharm Raja were in conversation the sage DURVASA came to the palace and told Lakshman that he wanted to meet Ram at ones. Lakshman did not allow him to go inside. Durvasa was very annoyed and threatened to destroy Ayodhya and to curse Lakshman but Lakshman did not bend as he was just doing his duty entrusted by Ram. Durvasa could not control his anger and he cursed Lakshman to leave the earth and instantly go to heaven. Then he opened the palace door himself and went inside. Ram was amazed to see Durvasa but he showed him full respect and served him well will food and drinks. The sage felt satisfied and told Ram about his curse upon Lakshman. Ram was unhappy to know that and told Durvasa that he had committed a grave mistake. Hearing this Durvasa went away in a bad mood. Then Lakshman came to Ram. He was quite perturbed and told Ram not to grieve for him. He then went to the banks of river Saryu and prayed to gods who carried him alive to heaven. Lord Ram and two other brothers felt great grief at the departure of Lakshman but were all helpless.

ramayana

45

Ram Leaves the World

Ram had already made up his mind to leave the world as his mission on earth was over. He crowned Lav and Kush and designated them rules of separate kingdoms. As Ram could not endure the separation of Lakshman who had left for heaven he too wanted to go the same way. Before his departure he wanted to crown Bharat as king in his palace. But Bharat wanted to accompany him. Ram then called Shatrughan who also insisted on going with Ram. Seeing their firm devotion, Ram agreed to take them along with him. They all then went to the holy river Saryu and plunged into the water. Brahma and all other gods appeared on the scene and carried Ram and his two brothers in a devine chariot to heaven. This is the story of RAMAYANA which brings bless and pleasure to the devotion who sing to verse with utmost reverence and devotion.

VALUE PACKS

LEARNING COURSE

COMPREHEANSIVE COMPUTER LEARNING

व्यक्तित्त्व विकास हेतु

CRASH COURSE

CONCISE DICTIONARIES

संक्षिप्त शब्दकोश

BUSINESS ECONOMICS DICTIONARY

Campus to Corporate

सम्पूर्ण आत्म-विकास

महिलोपयोगी

छात्रोपयोगी

SECURE A JOB

QUIZ TIME

मनोरंजन का ख़ज़ाना
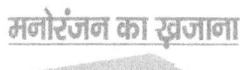

Contact us at sales@vspublishers.com

CAREER & BUSINESS MANAGEMENT
(कैरियर एण्ड बिजनेस मैनेजमेंट)

(Kannada)

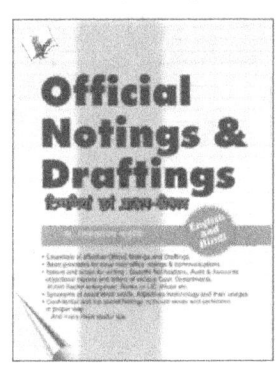

(Kannada)

STRESS MANAGEMENT (तनाव मुक्ति) | Audio Book

All books available at www.vspublishers.com

ALL TIME BESTSELLERS

PERSONALITY DEVELOPMENT
(व्यक्तित्व विकास)

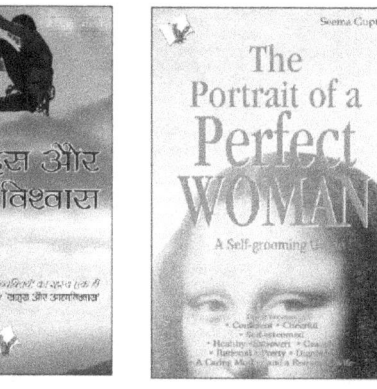

Contact us at sales@vspublishers.com

SELF-HELP/SELF IMPROVEMENT
(आत्म-सुधार/आत्म-विकास)

ALL TIME BESTSELLERS

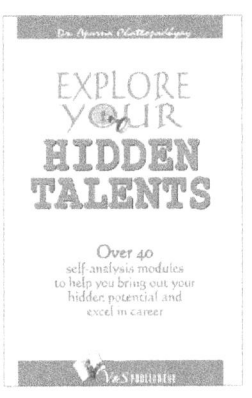

All books available at www.vspublishers.com

Quiz Books (प्रश्नोत्तरी की पुस्तकें)

ENGLISH IMPROVEMENT (अंग्रेजी सुधार)

      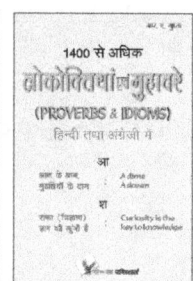

DRAWING BOOKS (ड्राइंग बुक्स)

BIOGRAPHIES (आत्म कथाएँ)

     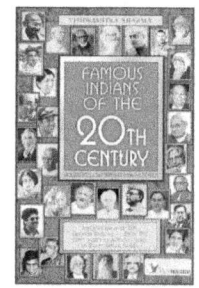

 QUOTES/SAYINGS (उद्धरण/सूक्तियाँ)

PUZZLES (पहेलियाँ) | COMPUTER | ACTIVITIES BOOK (एक्टिविटीज बुक)

   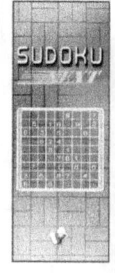    

Contact us at sales@vspublishers.com

POPULAR SCIENCE (लोकप्रिय विज्ञान)

CHILDREN'S ENCYCLOPEDIA
THE WORLD OF KNOWLEDGE

Code: 02147 P • Price: ₹ 800

MISCELLANEOUS

Set Code: 02122 S   Set Code: 12138 S

71 SERIES (71 श्रृंखला)

All books available at www.vspublishers.com

STUDENT DEVELOPMENT/LEARNING
(छात्र विकास/लर्निंग)

JOKES (हास्य)

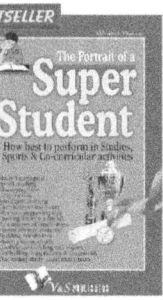   

COMPREHENSIVE COMPUTER LEARNING (CCL)

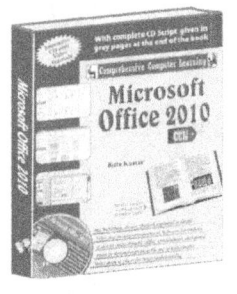   

Contact us at sales@vspublishers.com

HINDI LITERATURE (हिन्दी साहित्य)

TALES & STORIES (कथा एवं कहानियाँ)

All Books Fully Coloured

MUSIC (संगीत)

MAGIC & FACT (जादू एवं तथ्य)

MYSTERIES (रहस्य)

All books available at www.vspublishers.com

www.ingramcontent.com/pod-product-compliance
Lightning Source LLC
Chambersburg PA
CBHW080553230426
43663CB00015B/2828